D1387565

WAR

John Vetterlein

Bloomington, IN Milton Keynes, UK

WAR

First published by AuthorHouse 3/13/2007

ISBN: 978-1-4259-7447-3 (sc)
ISBN: 978-1-4259-7448-0 (hc)

Printed in the United States of America
Bloomington, Indiana

Cover design and all illustrations by the author.

[First published in 2005 by Spring Ast LIX
as a paperback entitled *WAR II* and distributed
privately at the sole discretion of the author.]

This book is printed on acid-free paper.

Throughout Europe and Asia, in North Africa and North America, wherever those who survived chose to put up a sign in remembrance, the war memorials and memorial plaques listing the military and civilian dead have the power to make sane people doubt the sanity of the world.

A History of the Twentieth Century, Volume Two: 1933 - 1951, Martin Gilbert.

Dedication:
To the misplaced persons of this planet and the innocent victims of war.

Contents

Explanation

In 1999 I published a collection of my poems on the theme of war under the title *War*. This was in two parts. Later, in October 2003, I re-published this work with additions and called it *War II*. Both sets were distributed privately.

It was my intention to produce *War II* in a hardback version for general sale. As a result of the invasion of Iraq by the USA and its allies, notably Britain, I had to rethink the presentation for the hardback edition so as to include some later work.

The present collection, again titled *WAR*, includes under a single cover not only the poems from the earlier editions of war poems, but also four single poem publications in addition to the short compilation, *Cenotaph*. This accounts for the sectional nature of the presentation. The cover pages from the original productions have been incorporated into the book.

The foreword from earlier editions has been retained intact since there is little I should wish to add or that I could usefully improve upon.

John Vetterlein
Orkney
June 2005

Introduction

The use of the word *war* today is ambiguous. The recent occupation of Iraq by members of a coalition led by the USA is frequently referred to as an act of war. It is hardly that when the world's most powerful nation militarily sweeps into a country which is unable to offer any effective or meaningful resistance. Some call such an act a turkey shoot.

Matters military dominate our so-called civilization. Venture into the British countryside on any weekday and you are almost certain to encounter some form of military exercise. Intensive low-flying training has been going on there for several decades.

The Ministry of Defence in cahoots with NATO ensures that vast resources are poured into the military. It is all very high tech stuff but most of it is about keeping a vested interest in motion. Military policy is shrouded in secrecy but it needs no high intelligence to work out that supersonic fighter jets have nothing to do with protecting us against terrorism.

These poems allude to war in this broader understanding of the word.

John Vetterlein
Orkney
June 2005

Foreword

To the extent that many poets have taken the theme of romantic love for their poetry, I have held with similar tenacity to the subject of war. Indeed, it could be said, quite justifiably, that war occupies my thought in a great deal of my work. This may be an inevitable consequence of my own World War Two experiences which in part led to my working in civilian hospitals for the period of my National Service between 1956 and 1958.

Obsession, unless it is channelled and controlled, (almost a contradiction in terms - non est, nisi est) may become self-destructive - like war itself. It would be equally true to say that the norm in human relations is to be at *war* rather than to be at peace.

The great musician and pianist, Artur Schnabel (1882 – 1951), in his long essay *Music and the line of most resistance*, rounding off, spoke of the breeding of an amazing average cleverness and many-faceted ignorance. This he foresaw might lead us into a preoccupation as a race with all manner of disastrous indulgences, including drugs and what he aptly called artificial eccentricities. None of this could be thought of as a happy state for human evolution to have arrived at, and yet here we are, besotted with materialism, doped on cheap and multifarious entertainment, soaked up to the eyeballs in the world-wide web information bonanza.
Stefan Zweig (1881 - 1942), writer, poet, thinker and man of letters, in the preface to his autobiography, *The World of Yesterday*, admitted to not being very proud of having written about himself. But thank God he did. Living through both World Wars, he experienced what he felt to be the extremes in individual freedom and celebration: at times hounded and trapped, at others lauded; and by turn despised for being a Jew. He would observe that it was his lot to be of a generation which had sunk into the ultimate degradation, where wars led mankind into the most bestial acts of violence and depravity - something which he hoped future generations would not allow to happen. Alas, such forlorn hopes. Zweig - who, along with his wife, took his own life - was not cognisant of the nuclear dimension in warfare. He may not even have had the scientific acumen to foresee the limitless possibilities technology places at the service of the merchants of war.

Such a climate has all but swept the planet clean of minds like those of Schnabel and Zweig; for, surely, how could they have tolerated it without crying out with all their breath at every moment of the day? Yet protest from our intellectuals and thinkers today barely reaches a whimper, so deafening is the silence.

Now, as we hasten towards a calendar landmark (the millennium, and no landmark at all in any real sense), I perceive a world decidedly rank and denuded of true purpose; a materialistic world, a world in which lies and falsehoods are tendered as truth by self-opinionated bigots both large and small; a world in which those in power, politically or otherwise, appear quite powerless to govern sanely at all. The nuclear weapon appears not to have convinced us of the folly and futility of war.

Therefore, what hope is there for a change of mind and of coming to our senses? Of course, what is required is a change of heart as well as a change of mind. But then, we are in the hands of those who appear to see human conflict only in terms of "an eye for an eye".

If war is to be regarded as a necessity, in the way that major surgery might be seen in the context of a human malady, then surely one is entitled to look forward to recovery at some stage? Or (absurdly) are we to take the analogy further and to see the death of the planet in terms of the inevitable death of the human body? To make the analogy complete, one would have to place the patient back on the operating table and for him/her not to recover from the surgeon's knife. This final visit to the operating theatre we may call the final nuclear theatre of war.

John Vetterlein
Orkney
1999

Index of Titles

Prologue

War?

What is war?

War is what we do when we call it war.

War is, above all, killing;
killing each other,
killing animals,
killing plants;
killing, killing, killing;

remember that,
war is about killing
no matter how we justify it,
no matter how unavoidable
(but war is an intentional act),

no matter what,
war is about destruction,
carnage, pain and misery.

What more is there to say?

Part I

Upon the king!, let us our lives, our souls,
Our debts, our careful wives,
Our children, and our sins lay on the king!

William Shakespeare: *King Henry the Fifth*

For the sake of form

For the sake of form,
let us have partition -
good to the right,
bad to the left,
warriors in white,
warriors in black -
and so, arranged thus,
let battle commence.

War III

War clogging the arteries of life,
war lying across all avenues we take,
takes all, sweeps all before it, war
the all-consuming human passion;
war, the forum for bravery and gallantry,
feeds where it consumes, assumes
the proportions of a starved,
rampaging monster,
has us at its beck and call.

Prepare for war

"Prepare for war"... the slogan goes;
scratching our bums as the planet burns.

A year to remember - a tribute to three musicians

I am born into a year
when Toscanini is preparing *Fidelio* with Lotte Lehmann,
and soon Europe is to plunge into another war
that will quickly engulf the entire world.

People will be hounded and displaced -
musicians and tradesman alike -
for no other reason than that they are Jewish;

Rachmaninoff will not have much longer to live,
and in that self-same year as I take my first breath
gives us his desolate *Third Symphony*.

Spot the difference

I ask myself, what separates us from
all other creatures of this planet?

Most things, most ways come up
with some sort of an answer,
for one thing, our crude predictions
and expectations - do the others
speculate and objectify?

Two things stand out from the rest,
gluttony and vanity; a plethora
of bits and pieces, devices, clobber -
all the fancy trinkets with which
we surround ourselves
to buttress our existence.

Other animals, by comparison,
take what is on offer. The factory
of an ant, for example, is an assimilation
of matter in cycle. Animals thrive in situ,
mankind fouls and mutilates. And for another,
our certainties (our sure-fire approach),
no matter how grotesque, the "there is no other way",
an arsenal of explosives fit for a stellar core - all this
and more, like: "God made us in His own image,"
and so...?

Jobs

Jobs, jobs, jobs - jobs at all costs,
jobs above all else,
Job must be turning in his grave.

The trade in arms comes first,
comes first in every sense,
its only rival - trade in sex.

Morality? the purist's joystick, a dictionary entry,
something to occupy the textbooks.

Intellectualizing cruelty

Along with all other propensities
came the propensity for cruelty with knowledge,
a new dimension to cruelty not shared
by the other living creatures of this planet.

Invention's praise!
(Know you this hell they have the gall to call civilization?)

They're flush with weapons out there in Albania and elsewhere,
fisticuffing it out with *Kalashnikovs*;

O what fame, to have your name writ upon so many corpses.

Cutting down to size

Take away their uniforms,
strip them down to their flesh
(share a nakedness with the refugees
their warring actions make);
range them in their nakedness
upon a frosted wire fence,
then invite them to wage
their futile, petty wars.

Black ink running through the snow

Human history, a sort of willy-nilly,
one day soldiers fighting and killing each other,
next, at Christmas, foes dancing together in the snow.

War is a sore

War is a sore.

In common with most other sores
we find it impossible not to pick at it.

The festering that is war will break all other sores,
bring about a gangrenous precipitation
causing all limbs to fall away
in a glorious putrefaction.

Bravery?

They said they knew no fear in the end,
so much repetition of the dehumanizing
deadly mission - shooting things out of the sky;

you have a job to do and a number assigned to you to get on with it;
thinking about it won't down the enemy,
thinking only makes you stink your pants.

World in conflict - nuclear style

Tricky one this, what to do
when all else fails.

Pull up the floorboards,
dig up the foundations,
bring down the entire house
upon the lot of us - Samson-like.

Come - the millennium?

And so, we must not be too emotional (about some things),
we must see it as the essential resolution
to the ending of the *Second World War*,
the destruction of Hiroshima and Nagasaki with atomic bombs
released by the United States Army Airforce.

And so we must think of ourselves,
the race of humankind, as having made progress
fit to celebrate a millennium pivoted on a notion
of Christ the Messiah.

We are entitled to congratulate ourselves
for seemingly having abolished slavery from trade
(we no longer send children down mines and up chimneys
not here in the so-called West at any rate),
all such things, as with our wars,
take place elsewhere in the world, beyond our front door.

We no longer burn people at the stake,
we electrocute and poison them instead,
and instead of the pocket handkerchief battle fields
of Crécy, Edge Hill and Agincourt,
the entire planet is a battlefield continually under threat
from immediate nuclear obliteration along with all other devices of war,
the product of trade across the world.

All this we have to celebrate,
come the millennium.

In search of a solution or simply repetition?

What to do when your very own life is threatened
or the lives of those dearest to you are threatened,
what to do when that threat comes
from an unaccommodating source,
from those whose only actions are violent and ungovernable;
what to do in such circumstances
where the only practical way open is to meet force with force?

then it becomes a battle between two physical systems,
nothing more, nothing less (no matter how each justifies
to itself the *right*, for even within the deranged mind
may be found a form of *reason* for physical behaviour).

And so arising out of this confrontation of wills
we have wars, or at least giant fisticuffs
(for whatever dignity there might once have been
in the concept of a *just war*, justice and ethics
have been left far behind).

Call it war, then;
war is the answer to our question;
an answer, a reaction - not a solution.

Mr Remuneration

Mr Remuneration, a chap with a job to do,
does his job to the best of his ability,
helps plan the procedures leading to
the blasting to smithereens.

Working in a *Ministry of Something* - a sort of institution -
makes it more cut and dried, bucks passing by the by,
holed up somewhere.

Thus Mr Remuneration, trading in war,
passes time away until even he, as with the rest of us,
has to die and is no more, leaves to posterity
the scattered fragments from the job he had to do.

Baghdad eulogy - grotesquery?

The *darts* that have flown our skies
in their millions now over the years
put their skills into practice,
unleashing destruction in the city of Baghdad.

"Air strikes", a little term to describe
missiles and bombs released from a distance
(by personnel, be it noted, doing a fine professional job
and for which we should be grateful),
delivered to the people of Baghdad
with love, from our Nation;
the only way to deal with a tyrant,
a parcel of experts will have you know;

all the well-worn rhetoric, the same old
well-worn techniques delivered with upgraded punch and precision.

What new word should they find for it?
not battle, not war: - *grotesquery*?

At it again

Mr Hussein wants to play a gassing game,
it gives an excuse to the rest to join in.

The military machine winds up again,
more weapons jostling, all the paraphernalia
of a bishy-bashing, high-tech war.

Remembrance Sunday

Here on Remembrance Sunday
they hoist the flag upside down.

Down in Iraq, on the selfsame day,
they huff and they puff and they blow,
the military machine all set and ready to go.

Sempre

Tell me war is only a necessary expedient
(the boys would much prefer not to...).

Read the footage, see the films and videos,
scrutinize the full panoply of entertainment,
wars and battles galore, the more the better -

give it up? Never!

War and sex

War and sex on telly and video
outdo cakes in hot sales. Who says
we haven't become a licentious race?

Against the arm of God?

As we sow, so shall we weep,
weep a haul of sorrow for our folly,
folly whipped on by greed.

We may look back to a moment when
in sheltered rooms we made decisions
wrought of pride and arrogance,
taking the military option,
(spat-out words congealing to fire),
choosing not to see beyond the slaughter,
justifying such decisions by some contraption
worthy of the bigot.

And so we course on,
abandoning any recourse to ethics,
rest instead all faith in our fallibilities
set against the arm of God.

Battle

Battle is about smashing things up.

Whatever art there might have been
in the put-up battles of yore,
war has always involved the killing.

War today is about an *intelligent* species
putting all its guts and brains
into the business of destroying things - outright.

War games - a countryside elegy

Who is there to take a stand?
Not professors nor their students,
nor the pretty poets and musicians
who gather here each year for their festivals;
the tourists too in their thousands
appear insensitive to what is happening
(makes you wonder why they come here).

Scarcely an eyelid raised to the thunder
(their ears and eyes stopped up you think?)
as the war games go on
across the hills and valleys of this sacred land.

On manoeuvres

Word came round, the convoy would be passing by
on such-and-such a day, and on that day we would be there,
waiting on the pavement to see it pass and to wave them on,
the men in their uniforms packed into their high-slung vehicles,
camouflaged liveries, trailing their implements, their heavy guns,
the full paraphernalia of war.

Uniforms and the myth

Generals - men, really, in uniform - stand on ceremony to the death.
Admirals - also dressed to show what they are - salute the flag.

Extraordinary to think all these types, and more,
were once babes with talc, most likely, sprinkled on their bums.

View from Astraea

Passing by at Christmas this year,
nineteen-ninety-four, at visual magnitude nine-point-five,
I tell you what I see across the Earth:
wars and famine, a ghastly pall, a raging light,
traffic jams and endless plastic.

Instantaneity - Bergen-Belsen

The camera took it in at a single stroke
the corpses laid out, emaciated bodies - flesh and bone,
except, the lens fails to record the stench,
fails to bring to life the human degradation,
this monument to perversion and debauchery;
the camera freezes in the instant the nightmare tapestry,
aeons of human agony and torture.

Death trains

Hear the *silence,* backdrop to the grinding wheel
steel on steel, iron railway death-trap.

Christmas 1998

Christ, what a mess - call it Christmas?

Where to begin in assaying the awfulness,
(why bother - water off a duck's back and all that),

As a start take the logistics - a package
of "punch Saddam" (his people, at any rate), then
we'll fly across the globe for beer and sandwiches,
celebrate plastic in all its guises, a rash of warring activities –
all that military hardware and stuff
exported to perk up the balance of payments;

the cross in ashes, Christ debased, betrayed
in all the multiplicity at our disposal - Christmas,
what a travesty - come in hogmanay, call down ignominy.

Men with guns

Men with guns,
as it has been, *always* - only the means have changed.

Trapped by the camera lens
men standing, feet astride, brandishing their pitiless power;
the unarmed women, children and men - cowering, cast to the ground;
call it part of war, call it what you will,
this sad spectacle is the abiding message,
indecipherable.

The rose garden

Thinking back, there was something
totally unconvincing about that ornamental park.

Clayhall - the very name dreamed up by some town hall clerk,
small and oblong, symmetrical in shape almost to a fault,
serving a quite ordinary average housing estate;
very basic, well intentioned,
planted out with beds of wallflowers and dahlias;,
a small ornamental pond where lilies and dragonflies met,
a circular concrete pond where men and boys plied their model boats,
a trellis walkway and a rose garden,
the heavy weight of summer perfumes,
all stationed under a war-torn sky.

Makes it the more difficult for those who survived
to believe any of it ever happened.

Night raid II

The throbbing of those engines,
the Dorniers flying over us
on their way to bomb the docks;
the throbbing of their engines
reaching down and into my brain.

Stalingrad revisited - and so?

It went on television, the battle of Stalingrad,
fifty years on; and so we watch and listen,
but until the stench is thrown at us,
the pain of wounding and dying
with our mutilated bodies,
it means nothing.

Generals Paulus and Hoth,
assigned the task of taking Stalingrad,
faced their Achilles heel, whilst Hitler and Stalin
slugged it out from their headquarters, each vowing
to outdo the other - score, Hitler two, Stalin one -
little wonder Hitler was so boastful; but Chuikov's
incessant flow of military reinforcements
eventually halted the German advance.

When the ice flow on the Volga
entered the mighty fray, the German foot
began to flounder, and before November was through
the Soviets had completed an encirclement.

And so it went, advantage and counter attack
swinging upon the pendulum of mutilation,
dead for dead, advantage countered, lost and lost
but never won (only death draws a positive score).

continued..

And so it proceeded towards the bitter end, not for surrender
this repetitious blend of obstinacy and fanaticism,
and so it wound on, under instruction from the Führer,
his witless army fighting to the last man (to save a sulky face?);
on the German side close on a quarter of a million dead and injured,
men at arms. And of the rest - civilians? A statistic never registered.
So went the battle for Stalingrad.

Postlude:

A little more than fifty years pass,
war passes to the television screen for real.

The Gulf Campaign (as with the Falklands a few years earlier,
a new nomenclature for the same thing - war);
tracks in the sand of the desert, men injected up to the eyeballs -
anti-this, anti-that (no anti-war, you notice), to come home to roost
as something appropriately called Gulf War Syndrome.
War, you notice this time, this messy footprint we leave to posterity,

The day the flying bomb came

Our road used to run up to the little park
with its circular pond where we children sailed our model boats.

Another street lined with lime trees
their stunted trunks appearing like sentries
guarding the line of terraced houses
up and down each side of the road.

And then, one day, the flying bomb came
appearing suddenly in the blue of summer's sky,
turning on its stumpy cigar-like fuselage,
tilting its wings in a kind of salute -
we all thought it was up for us:
after the explosion (a noise like a giant pack of cards
all falling to the ground as one),
the dust went about with this wine-sap tang,
filling our nostrils, sinking to our lungs,
the trees standing like skeletons of ghosts
draped in our shredded, every-day things.

The V2 rocket

It came unannounced, except that
one's n^{th} sense gave warning,
nothing that could be acted upon.

The come-and-go of life dispensed
concisely, the rocket gave no time to argue,
it achieved obliteration resolutely, outright and complete.

Part II

War

War is madness,
War is contagion,
War gets the limelight,
War insinuates, brazenly - appeals to the macho,
(just as boys will be boys, war is war),

War on to oblivion.

Tin 'ats and all that

Tin 'ats and Thermoses, the A.R.P,
a stick of incendiaries along the length of Walton Street,
Mrs Okeford going into labour, and her at forty-eight,
unseemly, some said, others put it down to the war;
communal shelters and all that, funny things happen in war.

What is a child to make of it all?

The bombers

The Dornier, the Heinkel and the Junkers,
over they came, wave after wave of them,
droning on and on, to drop their deadly canisters,
retch the city into flame.

Wellingtons and others - what's in a name?
(our lot at any rate, doing the same);
it was tit for tat no matter who started it,
no matter the rights and wrongs,
death and destruction were the end result.

Postscript

Once the flying bombs started, houses all about
went down like a pack of cards - and the rockets?

Targeted short of London, we were told much later on,
(propaganda leaked as false information by our lot),
made us the bull's-eye for the first misguided
guided weapon of modern ballistic warfare.

The "refugees"

"Bombed-out" meant your home had gone,
along with all your possessions;
we had the clothes we struggled to stand up in,
children clutching their teddies and dolls,
and that other commodity,
the brave face we soon learned to wear.

Modus unicus

There is no other way,
it's a law of nature:
a goat for a goat,
a throat for a throat;
war, war and yet more war;

Modus unicus, modus unicus.

Slogan

The day they dropped the atom bomb they said:
"war's doomed"!
Shout louder, nobody seems to have heard.

Burning ourselves out

Whatever we turn to we turn it to war;
what's left of life is a sort of spin-off when war is done;
but war is never done, we see to that,
hell bent we'll all go down together,
a burning tribute to our creator.

A belated question?

Out of all this suffering - what?

Does it have to be gone through over and over again?

If so, to what purpose?
Shelling a city from a warship off the coast,
(and some of those who fired the guns
got quite carried away
in the heat and excitement of the fray)
all that's been done before;
people dying for the sake of dying - what else?

Mentioned in dispatches
(Omit the "I", the "me" from poetry - and?)

That fly in my tent, flitting, irritating
as I try to rest between battles;
the Sun, slipping down across the canvas,
the fly at last content to rest too, I lie
with the back of my head supported in my hand;

I stare into the apex of the tent and wonder why,
why we are doing this - fighting
(even at school we were trained to fight,
yet punished for fighting amongst ourselves),
wondering why we do anything at all, why?
Not just to get a mention in *DNB*, surely?
"saw action at the battle of..."

That fly is active again, action and activity;
now I have the advantage, the fly within reach,
I may swat it down with the other hand
and, that done, snatch a little rest before the next battle;
please mention us in dispatches, the fly - and *"I"*.

God, the counter to arbitrariness?

A deranged mind in a body runs amok,
kills young kids, then kills himself;
people in the news, the news-people call in,
say it was a wicked act, an evil thing,
words can hardly accommodate outrage and grief.

And while all that was happening in a cosy little place,
nuclear submarines (a potential for infinite carnage)
stalk the seas, willed on by us.

The evacuation

As a child one came to accept the disordering of things by grown-ups.
The war evacuation programme was no exception;
following a day waiting endlessly at railway stations,
with railway journeying thrown in for good measure,
came the final ignominy - an enemy air-raid
that first night at our destination.

My mother, who had accompanied me, migraine and all,
dropped her rucksack to the hard wood floor of the school hall
(where we had been billeted for the night);
she swore openly, a thing I had never experienced before,
"Shit and piles, this is enough...", and said with such venom,
had Hitler been within earshot,
the war would have ceased on the instant.

Instead, rummaging though her rucksack
and finding a smashed jar of malt jam seeping into our things,
my mother resorted to tears;
and I, a mere child, felt totally helpless in a hapless world.

Railway stations

What's this of railway stations I hear you speak?

Knew you them as I knew them then - cold, echoing
in the pre-dawn light, the sweated steam alighting everywhere,
locomotives with heavy responsibilities -
troop-carriers, breakers of hearts;
carrying on a war on the Home Front, secrecy abounding;

the railway terminus where histories collide,
hope simultaneously coerced and derided;
waiting endlessly at barriers,
steel whistles piercing the icy dawn;

the railway terminus with its emptying and filling -
we went there to have our dreams disembowelled - all of us,
just going along with it, as if there were no other way.

Waiting for Christmas morning

The lead up to Christmas was always lonely
with Father away at the war.

At school we made paper chains,
and bought sticky stamps for *Spastics*,
the small motif looking like a line-less telegraph pole
stuck in my mind for good.

Carols: *God rest ye Merry Gentlemen,*
       The Holly and the Ivy,
       Once in Royal David's City.

Christmas cards with their inevitable snowy scenes,
misleading and full of mock cheer;
waiting for *Father Christmas* - the most exciting time of all,
it seemed Christmas Eve would never come,
and when it came it seemed it would never pass
(reaching down to the foot of the bed in the middle of night,
feeling for the empty sock, finding sleep somehow, eventually);

Father Christmas appeared to know when to make his sally,
the magic of the stuffed stocking,
filled in a secret pocket of time
(a time known only to *Father Christmas*),
feeling its lumpy contours;
there would be an orange for sure,
and an apple, and a little bag of nuts maybe -
in those days of wartime austerity,
Christmas somehow held its own.

Welsh harmony

It was in the valley of the Usk in Wales, many years ago,
I first saw the elusive dipper darting through the glades,
at a time when mines were active all over, coal in the south,
up north, at Dylife, lead spoil leached slowly down stream
to the great falls above Pennant;
and slate at Blaenau Ffestiniog,
mountains upon mountains of the stuff.

It's different now, the mines are closed - coal in the south;
and in the north, the lead is long dead,
the slate lies in silent heaps beneath the noisy skies,
wherein military jets ceaselessly exercise for war.

Learned apprehension

Standing in the tranquil dawn,
a slender moment slotted into space and time,
late dawn of a winter's morning,
no traffic upon the road save a solitary cyclist
freewheeling down the gentle slope towards Sourin.

Not here yet
the rumble of the thundering jets
that drove me out of Wales,
(it will come, surely it will come,
just as surely as it will pass - man's
infatuation with physical power).

And as I stand in the silence,
my ears are loath to let me forget,
and forewarn, of the thunder below the horizon,
before the jets storm over.

Revolving power

Silent armies in their din
masquerading for peace and truth
no clashing by night in ignorance of the plan -
all human ingenuity goes in to make the machine
full-proof - stand a projectile on a pin, wipe out sin,
sell it to the people as a panacea, they've believed it before,
they'll believe it agin, and agin, until it's all over, the end for them;
then, in time, creation and evolution may get on,
though there's nothing to tell man won't be re-invented,
and on past performance, in perpetuity,
make the same scraggy mess of it.

By example, tit for tat

Who dares speak for a nation,
exploding bombs underground
as a gesture to a neighbour,
who does likewise - tit for tat;

by example, blindly following folly upon folly,
so brave - nothing lacking,
save a bit of imagination.

Extinction (II)

Gales thrash new saplings to the ground,
Mars retrograding in Leo,
men pounding out each other's brains,
earthquakes reducing cities to rubble,
men in nuclear submarines
prepared to reduce all to nothing.

Word-capped trash

Word-capped trash, tongues useless, warbling;
treaties meaningless, as fragile as the paper they are written upon,
signatures hollow, impotent against tyranny and oppression.

Still waiting

Still waiting for a change of heart?
The realists - the self confessed ones - say,
You're living in cloud cuckoo land, the reality is:
Men are bastards, cannot keep their word,
Not in love, not in war - O!, to be so happy, so confident
In what one says, as happy as the pragmatists appear to be.

Modern war

Microchip precision guides the missile true,
burns Arthur to a cake, makes a pretty picture
for the camera to send home via satellite;

war, a spectator sport since the *Gulf*,
has all the players as of yore
but with the lights turned up.

Lotteries and land-mines

Were the chances even, triggering a land mine
as against winning the *National Lottery*;
in both senses, your number's up -
down with your soul - and your body?

Circuitous argument, this; I'll try it all the same:
trade is jobs and jobs is lives, equally in the balance;
who would I sooner have to make explanation to -
a guy without a job, or a father whose child, or wife, or...
blown to smithereens by one of your accursed mines?

Life's a gamble with diminishing returns,
once you step into the profiteering, gambling arena.

The good boys at play

Roar, roar, roar - war, war, war;
nothing has changed except that
we make more noise about it now.

Roar, roar, roar - war, war, war,
perhaps we don't even care any more?

B-52

Slicing-up the B-52s with a giant guillotine –
the ultimate ignominy?

The giant, eight-engined bombers, three-hundred-and-sixty of them
(almost one for each day of the year),
each capable of carrying a nuclear payload able to close all our days.

These monsters, presently obsolete, are being scrapped,
what takes their place?

Whatever takes their place,
nothing has changed in the minds and hearts of men,
still hell bent on mutual destruction.

In Civvy Street

In Civvy Street with war done down to dripping,
I'll dance my lassie home for good,
and have her drenched in kisses.

Mournfully, in C sharp minor

It would be audacious to say
one is expected (in this crazed world)
to carry on as if there were a vestige
of normality to it all, that would assume
an interest and people are mostly disinterested;

the harum-scarum that drives me up the wall
affects them not at all.

And so I turn my thoughts back
to my kindred spirits, imagine what Haydn
would make of all the din, aircraft screeching,
traffic thundering through day and night
(our determination to kill off night).

Brahms, I fear, on one of his country walks
assailed by a military jet, would never hear
his frogs croaking mournfully in C sharp minor.

And all those creative artists for whom
the unmolested environment was their inspiration,
would they cry out against the indignity,
would they allow their intelligence to be insulted,
or would they crawl underground,
shut up like a clam?

Glass blowers

Still evenings, windless - quiet,
you'd hardly know there was a war in progress,
refuse dumps smouldering happily,
the dank singeing cocktail mass permeating the air,
a sort of beckoning to the young adventurers;
young boys stabbing into the combustive depths,
rods of glass-tubing found scattered about the place
(the discardings of some laboratory,
some works where grown-up things happen),
then pulling free the gently glowing,
plasticized "inner end" - twisting, coiling,
blowing down tubes against the fumes,
improvising fantastic shapes,
contorted emblems to the war.

Somehow - demobbed

On demobilisation, following the war,
my father went up to London to fetch his "Civvies"
(a new suit of clothes with which to brave the world).

"In Civvy Street", they somehow put it,
(and I imagined this man who used to be my father,
and squaring him up with the man before me in his "Civvies"),
and lo, there was another image with which to play hide-and-seek.

There was this man, my father, somehow diminished -
shrunken by the war, looking for himself
(the mirror must have been a disappointment to him);
indeed it was a time to be dizzied -
we'd all been spun round so many times
we'd lost the will to count - to count on anything -
somehow coming to rest, eventually, soberly,
not quite knowing which way we faced.

Taking up the threads after the war

By degrees my father took up some of his old interests,
chess and lawn bowls;

I accompanied him on his tournaments,
I sitting alone on hard wooden seats in the lukewarm summer light,
watching the slow course of each black globe make its way,
first this end up, then the other...
there was something cathartic about it,
watching my father strolling up and down,
it was as if the strain of war were slowly draining from him.

In the interests of the State

Bob and Ed, well on in years,
hark back to their army days -
look forward to a reunion
with the boys from the regiment.

Great days, they were - bayonetting
practised with a sand bag, sticking the blade
right through until it came out the other side
(you have to imagine the blood and bursting entrails).

At the reunion, white wine and roasted pork,
Ed reminisces about the girl he had in Cork;
Bob, less forthright, goes for the caviar instead,

"Remember that time in Port Said?"
Great days doing as you were told,
doing it in the interests of the state.

Idle boot

The fighter planes, *pencilling* their trails
high up in the once, clear blue sky;
one way of idling time away,
no more nor less worthwhile, maybe,
than scattering molehills with an idle boot.

The air show

It was a promise, after what we'd all been through,
a day out on a Sunday, a visit to the annual air show;
we needed a break and everybody else used to go:

watching the giant, man-made birds in their stiff postures
hurtling through the air just above our heads - *exhilarating*
one young man told me in later years (one of those chaps
from the Air Ministry - The Ministry of Defence, same meat
different gravy - whose job it is to tell you what's good for you).

"For the good of the country" a schoolmaster said,
so it must be true; sandwiches and hot coffee from a Thermos,
crane flies in their thousands rising from the turf
in mock imitation of the ghastly air machines,
and to think we paid in cash to witness all this;
crass? or simple, unalloyed untarnished adolescent high spirits?

So close to the war ending,
you'd have thought we'd had enough.

Reckoning

Fifty years on
both parents gone
what are we left with?
Nothing - just the hydrogen bomb,
and wars, of course.

Little has changed.

Marcia funebre

The church bells stopped in their ringing
by bombs raining down from the sky,
this alone did not signify the onset of war,
war was there from the beginning of the beginning.

The musician on his rostrum
directing the players set out before him;
this assignment no sooner started, then ended;
all the players departed,
the music plays on - *marcia funebre*.

The status quo

Beneath the status quo
(do not rock the boat, folks),
all hell let loose,
so many escaping genies,
so many overturned bottles.

Life, the play, our planet the stage,
all writ down for the record,
records locked away in dungeons of secrecy;
speak condescendingly of protesters,
(much better to be wise from the comfort of your armchair);
move nothing lest you trip the slide to ruin;
moreover, crucially, enjoy ourselves steeped in apathy:
slide from war to war.

The journey we have made

We can see the journey we have made
from cross to nuclear bomb
from Palestrina to *Spice Girls*
from Michelangelo to sheep's heads drenched in formalin
from loam meadows to sanitized fish cages
from pyramids to millennial domes
from clear, star-studded skies
to milk-white, exhaust-spewed haze
from silence to bedlam
we can see the journey we have made.

To the very edge

You may not hear the words above the din,
the words they use to justify the sin;
those who perpetrate the slaughter
attempting to dignify their actions;
call it war, call it what you will,
what now happens under the banner of war,
has more to do with violence for violence sake.

The wraps are off,
the violence seen for what it is,
even so it makes little difference,
men indulge to the very edge.

The last supper

Calmly over supper, to an audience of chosen guests
(dissecting his delicately prepared cooked fish the while),
our host informs us *hydrogen bombs* are necessary
to keep the bear from the door::
"You really think so - it'll never be used?"
"No, never."
"And if it were to be?"
"O! God forbid."

How 'tis to be *useful* without use escapes logic, but still,
I undertake to inform, without actually speaking for God:
"Such awesome destructive power, this *bomb*,
quite outside any sense or comprehension."

All this is of little account, I'm told:
"Things once invented cannot be un-invented - be realistic, now."
"No, not un-invent - true: rejection?
We have free will, we may still reject an evil?"

Our host's response to this observation, is to pat his serviette,
then to pour another glass of clear, red wine.

Part III

War I

War is no more, nor
no less than
our collective nemesis.

The hate trap - dust to dust

The hate festers like hate.

The killing machines take over,
machines against the flesh;
flesh-exploding missile carriers
take the war to the core -
the suicide bombers in endless conflict
with high-tech, hard cased weaponry.

I recall as a boy in the Second World War
being taken to the scene of an aircraft crash,
an enemy plane brought down
and falling on a cinema. Only last week
we watched the Gaumont British News
dishing out war propaganda in there.
Now I was watching as people thronged
to glimpse the piece of German meat
spattered on a wall still upright in a sea of rubble.

I had no idea then that what I was witnessing *was* normality;
the peace we supposedly craved and fought for,
no more than a breathing space
between the sustained conflict of souls.

The lure of flame

The talk is of war, but war is simply a word;
what they contemplate is more destruction and killing.

They have the instruments
(built out of a contagion for violence),
therefore their use is inevitable,
inevitable as the fate towards which
we spiral as moths lured towards the naked flame.

War, war, bloody war

September: a painted-lady from Biscay
dances across the heather slopes
here on Rousay.

September, all the talk is of war;
war - I ask you - we go to war?!
war, war, bloody war.

September, the apples ripen
leaves of the aspen turn pale and fall,

September, and all they think about is war;
war, war, bloody war...

War II (with an apology to Edgar Alan Poe)

War to end war?
no more war?
"Never more,"
quoth the raven,
"Never more!"

World War Four

They marked the ending of *World War Two* in two phases,
a celebration marking the signing in Europe of _ ,
and several weeks later, the war in Asia
terminated following the two atomic bombs
released over cities in Japan -
several hundred thousand more lives
wiped from the face of the earth.

How many millions slaughtered
in the space of a handful of years?

And since then, nuclear proliferation,
and so many wars world-wide
makes talk of a "Third World War"
as meaningless as the concept of a *fourth*.

War...?

The eternal question

Live and let live, or
kill or be killed?
This is the eternal question.

The physical fact is plain for all to see,
extinction is in the hands of the exterminators,
not to hold against them, plain suicide.

The request may go out all the same:
live and let live
is a formula of unquestionable merit,
given the chance.

The machines we have made

A dead lady, over one-hundred years old,
is transported to her resting place on a gun carriage:
guns firing a salute.

Across the world,
men, women and children are being gunned to death,
aircraft bomb, missiles explode,
there is a reign of machine terror;
this terror is perpetrated by all sorts and conditions of men;

we are machine driven,
we drive our machines in a non-stop orgy of violence:

the machines we have made, have made a hell.

Means to an end?

The end's in sight but never gained.

Our lives are our practices - the things we do;
most based upon whim or some illusive goal;
and wars, for whatever cause, are fought
because that's what we do - wars upon wars,
destruction and want,
and because the end is never achieved,
the means and the end become one and the same.

Sad world - war, a postscript

It was better then - we got by;
school seemed hard, things *were* hard just after the war,
no pocket money, any money that came my way
was gleaned through generous uncles,
aunts, a friendly godmother.

It was exciting to make "funds" stretch,
one was readily satisfied, delighted
simply to hold something afforded
from such small stock - building up slowly
a collection of Waterman's coloured inks,
coloured pencils, rough-papered colouring books,
a small box of Harbutt's Plasticine.

Today's kids go for mobile phones -
little wonder some of them "graduate" to drugs.

Sad world.

Face the facts

Where to begin - how will it all end?

Start with this lavish little booklet - *The Moray Firth Aviation Trail*
(cover page bristling with the paraphernalia of modern combat,
back cover page, a sweet female thing advertising *cashmere knitwear*),
a joint effort from the British MoD and the Scottish Tourist Board,
an unlikely brew of blast to smithereens and chocolate sponge cake -
propaganda at its most potent, wolf-in-sheep's-clothing approach.

Travel page by page, savour the juxtapositions:
Nimrods in flight, Kinloss Abbey burial ground,
Tornado fighter bomber bisecting the Old Man of Hoy,
Buccaneer low flying, nosing into Crash Memorial, Lossiemouth,
the good old Spitfire tilting over a solitary memorial cross,
Mosquito from Bamff attacking in a Norwegian fiord, spring 1945,
Banff Strike Wing Memorial stone set in pristine countryside;
and so it goes, no change - no hope?

Face the facts. Does anybody seriously suppose
there could ever be a dismantling of all this aggressive hardware,?
All those jobs, all those hard-headed trained-up guys and dolls?
Be honest with yourself, even in a cosmos full of aeons,
can you really believe man will kick the habit?

The planet is doomed; as custodians, we have failed,
no point in pretending otherwise; there's only one formula we understand:
"The fist is mightier than the tongue."

Face the facts, mankind is destined for a sticky end -
it's only a question of time.

[With acknowledgements to the United Kingdom Ministry of Defence,
and the Scottish Tourist Board.]

Prospect

The military way is the only way,
"It has to be done that way," they say.

My single response has to be:
"If that is your submission,
it's a bleak outlook for humanity."

Hopeless - I

Today I felt how hopeless it all is.

As I waited for the funeral procession to arrive
a military jet hurtled over our heads;
remarks from a dapper little fellow:
"I'd give my right arm to be up there"
opened up the hopelessness of it all;
indeed it is hopeless,
and I feel impotent as usual,
helpless and hapless and ready to leave.

No title III

There is no solution, no healing
only the non-stop killing and maiming.

They fought and killed and got killed, countless injured,
and in the infinite mingling and mangling
I am still here to mourn, to be constantly reminded,
revisited by the nightmare, to watch and listen.

Christmas passed again,
the bombing and killing goes on,
on and on, and on...

Next year there'll be a message on a card telling me:
"We visited so-and-so ...", meaning, they took off
and flew over land and sea, a sort of holiday
visiting these death hell-holes, all contributing
to the great commercial oil rag burning,
releasing more noxious fumes into our beleaguered atmosphere.

There is simply no answer, no solution,
we just go on tapping each other off the board.

The practical approach

Bomb them dead from a great height,
bomb them as we did before,
rain down death in hundreds of thousands of tons of high explosives:
bomb, bomb; bomb in anger and in retribution, for whatever reason,
go on doing it as the only practical option.

The history of man

Was it really ever as it was,
as I seem to see it in my memory?
the Windrush flowing gently
by the streets of Boughton,
clouds heavy with summer's
soft drenching drowsiness,
making everything feel lazy and endless?

Was it ever as innocent as it seemed?
despite the war, larks sang on,
filled the sky with their trilling.

As well to make something out of it,
methinks, no matter the make-believe,
better than the reality, the agony and the suffering.

The history of man is the chronicle of slaughter.

Twenty-first century reality

Reality in the twenty-first century
follows the old, cold reality:
force persecution politics,
but with a "brave new ingredient" -
regime change banged out
through the "bunker buster".

The war years

We went though all that
just so that men could behave badly
later on.

The dusk of civilization - a miscellany

Cold mutton, cold war, cold comfort.
The Western powers are fighting for the very survival of civilization.
President Whistleblaster toasts the mission
in flight at *two mac* fuelled by wine at £300 a bottle.
"Absolutely."

Question: What is the position on the ground in Afghanistan?
"Pock marked and on the run."
Looks like things are moving, then?
"Absolutely."

Tell me, Mr Expert,
what will General Schwimakarhamandin be doing?
"Running amok, most likely."
Raping and pillaging - par for the course?
"Absolutely."

At home, in the fresh fields of civilization,
two kids set fire to a drunken tramp,
(worth a mention); hot potato: absolutely.

Halloweens of the dusk, a grenade through your window,
more exciting than flour and used engine oil.
"Absolutely."

Continued…

Civilization seen through a dust storm:
ambassadors in fart-free trousers,
looking for a tart for the night,
get it in whilst there's still time - absolutely!

Anything much to look forward to?
"Everything."

"Absolutely"...

In touch - out of touch

Our worlds touch and overlap,
then separate. Life is about loss,
loss of innocence, loss of family;
we do our best to turn it into a celebration,
but no honest person is fooled.

Bitter sweet, sweet and bitter,
the sweetness and the bitterness
are indistinguishable
one from the other.

The nomad, modern soldier
kitted out with the latest hand-held weaponry,
face bristled, fag wobbling between the lips;
touch and destruct - what real hope is there?

The lessons of history

Did any of us seriously believe
we'd learned anything from the experience of *the* war?

Could we really begin again and make a better job of it this time?

If we truly believed it then,
since then we have failed to pass on the message.

Today the mess of war, along with most things,
is worse than it has ever been
and is getting worse.

Across the great divide - the age of innocence

What difference is there between inevitability
and the notion that our lives are non-negotiable?

Once they had cracked the atom
and opened up the great divide,
what future was there to follow
but this one - the road to hell?

Before the war, before the great divide,
who would have guessed?

The men with their secret power;
they must have known what they were letting us in for;
we, the ordinary people, went about our business and our pleasures:
a day trip to Hemingford Grey, punting along the Great Ouse,
back home along the Great North Road;
seems, looking back, across the great divide,
a twilight time, our age of innocence.

Postscript:

We tried it again soon after the ending of the war,
went down in Mr Sunnex's Humber Super Snipe (the entire family of us),
but it was not the same - the bottom had fallen through.

War, just petering out

The war came to an end in an unpredictable sort of way:
we had been expecting it, it was only a question of time,
time filling up with the dead -
men killing one another to the bitter end;
one war's end, another still running,
others just about to begin, others still running on,
wars run on and on, the show never stops.

But, where it had just closed for us,
we found ourselves in a state of suspension,
not knowing quite how to apply ourselves,
at something of a loss under quiet skies without threat.

I went out into the countryside on my father's cycle
(sat astride the crossbar, the saddle sticking in my back)
in search of the promised land; it was a time like no other
(just thinking about it creases the mind, quivers the spine).

Where did it all evaporate to?
For the promise was never found,
only the memory of hope lingering for a time before vanishing -
nothing ever is ever as it seems,

and yet?

An exercise, code name "Firepower"

Ladies and gentlemen of the profession,
we are gathered here today to plan an exercise in armed combat
(better that than war, war may come later, but for the present___).

Ranked: men and women of the profession,
here we are of our own volition, in it together,
comrades in arms, comrades like no other,
stick to each other through thick and thin -
has a ring to it, don't you think?

On one point, are we all agreed to our purpose?
We are. Thank you. We have a job of work to do -
full stop!

Higgins (a fighter pilot) enjoys his flying, likes his badges,
is proud of his wings and in his uniform looks immaculate,
clean and to the point, passed and ready for the attack;
when there's a job of work to do, you get on with it,
thankful not to have to address the rights and wrongs
(all that goes by default where the end is clear);
when the end is clear the means take care of themselves.

Higgins will see it through like a gentleman,
and when he retires - God willing - he'll be thought well of,
served his country like a true scout: thumbs up;
one, two, over and out.

Wars

Wars - for what?
For what reason?
To satiate a human need?

Men will fight no matter what stands in their way,
they will defy the nuclear bomb itself.
(How dare anyone invent something so awesomely powerful,
it will take away our freedom, our freedom to fight).

Wars will rage on,
rage on against all reason, and in the end?

The end will speak for itself.

Doing for the doing

We have reached the toy age in which war's a game,
the pieces we knock about - those left out -
driven to the margins, beyond despair.

The toy age.
Computers amassing facts and stacking them for all we're worth,
represent the *Universe* as pancake, lemon meringue,
sprinkled with sugar and wobbling
in time to the beat of the non-stop pop.

In *Vodka City* they soak themselves silly,
play each other at dice (some things remain simple it seems);
a son in the service of *something*,
off with his bomber to bomb the guts out of a place
that was once part of the great *Union*.

Nobody accountable to anything - just doing;
without good or bad there is only nothing,
and nothing is easily served - you just get on and do your thing,
that's it - doing for the doing.

The Millennium - a toast

I give you - the status quo!
To accepting things as they are,
To horror as it is,
To what we have made of it,
To what we have learned,
To what we seem incapable of learning,
To all that we have invented and cannot disinvent
(even though rejection remains an option),
the wars we have started and can never finish,
To the endless trail of misery we cause,
To the fat men of industry and commerce
who feed off conflict and discord,
To all those who excuse what they do
because that's the way it's always been done,
To those who will not seek another way,
To all who say, "we go along with it",
To those who find it impossible to say NO!
My plea - there HAS to be another way.

War on the web

All the contours are smudged
into contours of the same information glory-hole;
aggression, pigheadedness, petulance,
small-mindedness, pomposity,
all rolled into one:

surf your way through the lot:
war on stage and in the theatre - war on the web.

Whist and rummy

We passed the time in the shelter at the start with whist and rummy

hearing the incendiaries whistling about outside,
damp air inside and out;

when the bomb came down with a thud

"When it's all over", somebody said ___

fifty years on and we're still waiting ...

Lost ethic

Mankind finally parted from his soul
somewhere in nineteen forty-four -
aerial bombing of cities reaching towards a climax,

but in post-war runaway productivity
(as epitomized in the motor industry),
craftsmanship is taken away from the hand,
custom-built replaced with mass production
(death through endless repetition),
the work without ethic or ethics,
set "free" in countless stillbirths.

Telepathy

I have to believe it if it's true.

A small boy, scruffy, sitting on a kerbstone,
resting with my head between my hands, dreaming;
the figure on the brain's margin
is Dad headed home on a forty-eight hour pass,
smart in his blue airman's uniform;

and it was so, for looking up I saw him
in the distance striding purposefully forward,
the event confirmed as he raised me
with his hands high above the ground,
high above his head.

Fate's unfolding

We fed off expectation
without any foundation for so doing;

it was a necessary delusion
to enable us to endure the horror of war;

one day father would return to us,
making our little family whole again;

but the earlier wholeness was an illusion,
my contribution as the child of a perfect union
was no less fated than the rest of it;

and for me the spectator,
to feel the fall of my progenitors,
came to be the driving force
in a life of personal failure.

Ely

They stumble and shuffle up the "hill"
their backs to the cathedral, white smocks
for the cloisters set as backdrop,
Belisha beacons in the foreground.

"Coming home" from the war,
how to describe it - exhausted, weary?
all our reserves stretched into the war effort,
it will take a decade or two - a generation -
to erase the down-at-heel image;
and that done, full pelt we'll go down the other avenue,
a culture built out of burning oil as fast as we can,
city cathedrals, islands of a bygone age, rising above the fumes.

Sharing the shelter with mother

Mother could not sit upright in the low-roofed Morrison shelter,
instead we lay huddled together listening (what alternative was there?)
to the droning of the bombers flying above,
the explosions from the bombs,
the pounding anti-aircraft guns,
the whistling of shells,
the cracking of the shrapnel raining down.

We listened and waited,
waiting without expectation or much knowledge;
(speculation may have run riot inside our heads,
but this was never spoken of, instead Mother prayed quietly);

and I would shut tight my eyes,
and dream of the days we had together
as a family, before father was called to the war.

The men of bomber command

The men of bomber command, the air vice marshal types,
have to be in a category of their own;
the way things have grown,
such men are essential to the status quo,
careers in mass killing.

But then, expect no more, no less;
products of the messy business of being
what we are and what we have made of it;
come too far along the twisted path
ever to find a way back: time out,
just a matter of time;
all the suffering through all the ages of man.

Handed in - this our final report;
all in, all out, all gone;

honours stand, statues lean (mildewed and green),
salute the men of bomber command.

By the worst means, the worst. For mine own good
All causes shall give way: I am in blood
Stepp'd in so far, that, should I wade no more,
Returning should be as tedious as go o'er.

Act III, Scene IV. Macbeth: William Shakespeare

The salute

On an aircraft carrier (one of the largest in the largest fleet)
somewhere, the president toasts the world to the mission complete
then opens a tin of sardines.

God replete in his sanctum,
and the brightest nation in the world
going higher and higher on a missile shoot -
showing somewhere in a town near you.

Men and women in suits and uniforms
there in the middle of nowhere just to receive the salute.

The same old track

Such weighty issues discussed
like, whether mankind has a future;
so much at stake
like, will the president land on his feet?
so much talk
that when it comes to action
there's only one track they follow - war!

There for eternity

Ward Lock Red Guide for Pwllheli,
photos from before the First World War,
scenes of docile innocence,
not seeing the awfulness of what lies ahead,
advertisements praising Empire and fortitude;
our glorious past, our prospering future,
the future our men in battle fought for;
we, one step still rooted in the past,
a lengthening stride for tomorrow.

It was all going to be all right -
fight the good fight,
God on our side, and all that.

And the British seaside resort, like the Empire itself,
there for our pleasure, there for eternity.

The destruction of life

Human life is the fusion of the physical and the emotional:

the trend is to stamp out the emotional
by placing all our emphasis on the physical;

we can only explore life in full through harmonizing
the physical with the emotional;

war is the extreme exercise of extinguishing the emotional,
through the destruction of the physical - the destruction of life.

The legacy of the 20th century

Trained to fight, trained to hate,
trained to kill and to be killed.

The silence of absence

There is nothing so powerful as the silence of absence.

At Christmas - absent friends - a traditional Western Christmas,
scenes of snow's gentle peacefulness, the season of good will,
a father "on leave from active service", expected home,
and then, the interjection, something else intervening:
"Whilst on exercise in _____", Christmases henceforth, empty;
a Christmas tree decked out and ever waiting:
"To Father, with love _____", the present without a presence.

There is nothing so powerful as the silence of absence.

Bomber's Moon

Full moon.
"Bomber's moon", they called it.
We felt naked, lying on a white table-cloth
just waiting to be picked off,
the bombers flying over in their hundreds
raining down their lethal canisters.

This is war, they told me,
having recently celebrated my fifth birthday
with a card from Dad somewhere in the country
learning to be an airman and, presumably,
looking up at the same moon.

The moon, indifferent to things being done
in her name, blazed from a sky
peppered with bursting lights and tracers,
all seeming futile and ridiculous in her presence.

This is war, as served up in the twentieth century;
but wait (four years), you've seen nothing yet:
Hiroshima, Nagasaki on the menu
being prepared on a side plate,
and served in a split-second flash of raging light
that will temporarily blind the moon.

Is it for real?

A sharp call summons me to the window:

a crow and a raven in mock combat - or is it real?
the raven, dancing, hovering above a fence post;
the crow raging in, wings flapping outrageously,
a poorly balanced combat it would appear - is it real?

And this war all the talk is about,
the world's militarily most powerful nation
going in and sorting out a rogue state - is it *really* war?

The crow makes off shortly,

the raven, settling firmly on the fence post,
preens himself.

The game of war

The players mass the field;
there are rules, but the rules, like the game itself,
are somewhat arbitrary and readily disregarded;

the rules admit the tidying up brigade,
identified appropriately by a badge - a cross in red;
a pity the argument cannot be extended,
an agreement not to have the game at all,
a rule to be honoured in the spirit and in the breach.

Vista Drive

They had an explanation for so many things it seemed,
why straw was laid in the road outside the house
of a very sick child - to deaden the noise of passing traffic.
What sort of illness? the child in me enquired;
an answer to that was not forthcoming.

There was so much from that quaint land of childhood
which escaped my understanding - all of it, I suppose;
childhood played through a dream,
(it was a dream as it was happening,
it is a dream as I recall it today);
unable to grasp quite what it had to do with me,
the bombs falling all about - why spare me?

Until the bomb fell that destroyed much of *Vista Drive*,
Vista Drive had been no more than another named street
(it was just around the corner from us);
the bomb turned everything inside out - dust on the outside,
bodies beneath, buried in the rubble of lath and plaster,
brick and tiles, shattered pipes, splintered glass.

The senselessness of it all became a common pattern,
eventually so familiar, so habitual as to imprint
its own peculiar smell of normality;
normal yet grotesque, grotesque and never unexpected.
And through it all a sense of anticipation,
fatalistic acceptance that when it came
the end would be the same as the beginning
in an arcane, improbable sort of way.

Debacle

It is morning, everything is still
following a night of storm and snow;
the hills lie as if abed, blanketed in snow;
the sun but scarcely risen
bathes everything in a peach-ochre glow;

the scene, just for a moment,
as it might have been ten thousand years ago,
soon to be taken over by the military for their daily run.

Day after day, week after week,
year in year out, they practice their deadly craft;
fighter jets, bombers and surveillance aircraft
scoring the sky with their hideous trails,
the air searing with the sickening roar -
bedlam - war, war, war.

What is war?

What is war?

War is what we do
because we cannot help ourselves;

war is what we prepare for,
therefore war becomes inevitable;

war is about destruction and killing;
war, for whatever reason,
delivers more war, not peace;

peace is what comes to those
we destroy through war;

war will only cease when
war has destroyed itself.

Back from a raid - captured on film

Cheers! Waves and thumbs up,
hats in the air, airmen, all smiles
on their safe return from a bombing mission -
the "thousand bomber raid" on Cologne.

What to read into this?
Rather, what response?

The message as signalled by Christ from the cross:
"Forgive them, for they know not what they do"?

Life - a madness

Our modern lives are a madness;
from fast (and not so fast) travel
to fast foods and ergonomics -
we're "up the creek".

Ministers of state fly furiously
round the world stoking up war and strife;
a self-imposed nightmare scenario made real.

What a Dante or a Milton would make of it
one can only guess at.

True freedom

I am "here" writing this I'm told
because others fought and gave their lives for freedom;
like most things, there is a grain of truth in what they say;
but I shall go on protesting against war all the same.

They would have us all join in;
our political "masters" push us into battle:
the same pattern will endure so long as we submit.

"Nobody wants war", the saying has it - what nonsense!
to pour such vast resources into something nobody wants?!

Better to die or to be killed than to be caught up in the killing.

True freedom visits only the departed from this earth.

No man can steal another from the self;
killing only degrades us all in life.

Death and war - a short meditation
(The party's over II)

Is death a testing of our vanities?

The thought that we are to disappear,
to be no more?

Is not the reflection of it enough
to demonstrate the futility of war?

So much a fear of extinction have we,
we extinguish all in our path for the party.

The changing face of war

They called it war
when men faced up to one another in battle;
battles led to slaughter and carnage,
fire and destruction - hell on earth;

not just the human participants
but all creatures and things, great and small.

War has *progressed* a long way since then,
from the men in armour charging at each other on their steeds.

The inventions we have made
have nearly all been turned to warring applications,
killing from a distance has travelled far
from the days of bows and arrows and muskets;
now automated technology does our dirty work
in vast orgies of killing and destruction;

sanitized and sterilized,
numbed brains press blindly on, regardless -

God pity our souls.

The universal sport

War, once the sport of kings,
now a source of employment
for the millions of minions.

Late cut - after the Second World War

With the war done at last
we kids played on - cricket on the hard, concrete alley floor
soon gave way to soft turf of the school playing fields
so long forbidden to us.

Who cared? No more air raids,
no more bombs; the world could move on to better things,
or so we thought then - it has not worked out like that of course.

Be all that as it may
(nothing can alter our foolishness it seems)
I look back from my position fifty years on,
savour the memories -
cricket on Brentwood's green and pleasant ground,
days of unhurried measure,
friends and family all intact,
wonderful, wonderful days in retrospect.

Hopeless - II

It is hopeless, hopeless, hopeless.

There's no future, there never has been;
we are ruled by ignoramuses;

the mass of people are apathetic,
indifferent to what is being done in their name -

It is hopeless, hopeless, hopeless.

The price of oil is rising;
the Chancellor squeals for more,
more, more, more - more oil to feed our gluttony,
our addiction, more oil to burn, more war,
more growth, more of everything -

It is hopeless, hopeless, hopeless.

The voices of protest go unheard and unheeded,
democracy is a sham; we elect tin-pot leaders
who then become tin-pot dictators,
government has about as much idea how to govern
as a rotted toothpick -

It is hopeless, hopeless, hopeless.

It is hopeless,
to pretend otherwise is to live a lie,
progress is founded on a lie,
we lie and fool ourselves on,
we are morally bankrupt -

It is hopeless, hopeless, hopeless.

A matter of perspective

An unprecedented demand.

A demand for what?

A disaster on an international scale,
an earthquake under the sea
and causing destruction and death
over a large portion of the globe;

corpses rotting in their thousands,
people missing presumed dead,
communities decimated.

A response?

The most powerful nations (militarily) of the world
cough up sums in aid, a mere fraction
of what they spend each day on war.

The cockle stalls - a solace of endings

The war done with, we made our way to the seaside,
a day out next the cockle stalls,
just the two of us, mother and me;
it seemed like paradise at the time -
the tension draining away with the tide.

It glows like a vision of paradise in my memory,
yet my mother's sad and solitary countenance,
together with my own sense of loneliness,
all fuse to make a memorial to despair.

I have made it into old age,
I have lived through it all,
and now all that is left
is a sense of utter emptiness,
a solace of endings.

Open question

Upon the king.

Upon us all falls the challenge,
whether to fall victim of the sword,
or principle denied,

all have died - for what?

Big business - bombs

The News: Sammy blew up Sammy
in a bus bomb somewhere,
and somewhere else somebody else
planted a bomb outside *Taylor's Good Time Bar*
and blew up Sammy and Jayne and all...

Planting bombs and dropping bombs
is all the go these days;

Chemical Ali, they say, poured petrol
down the gullets of his incinerated victims,
for which the USA invaded Iraq
dropping many thousands of tons of bombs.

Bombs are obviously big business now.

Doing it his way

Dear *Mr President*, you have all the aces:
the most powerful military machine
there has ever been - with no rival in sight.

You have no need of rules,
you may do just as you please;
if the water looks cold
then heat it up, impose your "god's" will
across the globe.

The incontrovertible truth

It is incontrovertible, the way it has to be done
even though we are constantly being "told"
nobody really wants it done that way;

more effort expended into ways and means
of blowing things up - men, women and children,
nature's fauna and flora - all enjoying a smashing time.

By today's standards - so what?

By today's standards Garbo looks dated,
Crawford painted (though surprisingly vivacious).
So what? An age that pastes itself to the nuclear banner
has nothing to crow about - dated? So what?

Modern war

Those who stake their future on the nuclear threat
(an outright destruction of the planet no less)
deserve all they get - that very destruction itself.

Final call

The curtain's coming down,

dragged down by our warring aspirations,
our distrust,
our greed, our arrogance,
our mealy-mouthed, corrupt
and pointless promulgations.

Our war machines
smash all before them -
all creatures great and small;

forgiveness?

God spare the meek,
the weak and the needy;

God care over all other species,
and what's left may go to hell.

***

Cenotaph

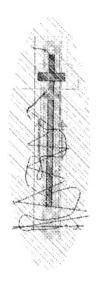

Their children also shall be dashed to pieces before their eyes;

Isaiah XIII

A proposition - a question

"Against the rules for the conduct of war",
or something of the sort, the actual words
appear irrelevant, not so our behaviour.

So, there is criminality even within war -
not war itself? Such arbitrariness.

Should not God, by being God,
forbid all war and warlike acts?

If not, why not?

Rules of Engagement

There are rules to war, you know,
like anything else; like anything else
you soon learn how to break the rules.
Never mind, as with the *law* (an ass, some say)
it is all rather fascinating.

The treatment of soldiers

Foe soldiers are the fodder
(like you).

In the killing
do it tastefully
with full military...
come at them hammer and tongs
with all the might
natty inventions give;
if in a night-raid, say
over so-and-so,
all sorts get maimed and killed,
spare a thought for the soldier
and decorate him, if appropriate,
appropriately.

War's a funny business

See this, it's called a uniform - wear it.
See this, it's a weapon -
we'll train you to use it.
See this, it's a prisoner;
there are rules about prisoners -
you mustn't abuse them.
Over there is the enemy,
mostly men like you,
in uniform and trained
to use weapons.
In between you'll find civilians,
they don't wear uniform.
When we capture prisoners
we imprison them,
they shouldn't try to escape,
but if caught in the act - shoot,
if caught on the run, well outside,
bring them back and lecture them.
You don't take civilians prisoner,
(it's more convenient to have them dead);
civilians are a bit of a nuisance
where war's concerned, as I say,
they tend to get in the way.

(Observing, in 1995, VE-Day of 1945 May 8)

Non est nisi est...

Sunlit apples drink to the dying day,
nettles play host to butterflies,
we, a universe apart, construct antipathies
and turn them into war.

Cenotaph

The voice of the "Unknown Soldier"?

They come to my tomb with their words
and their tributes, guns firing,
war 'planes over-flying.
They come to my tomb to remember
the countless dead fallen through war.

As they stand in silence at the Cenotaph,
wars raging all round,
nothing shakes their faith nor their spirit.
They will come and come again
to "honour" me, and between time
stir the potion that will ensure
there'll always be more bodies
to pile on top of mine.

Subterfuge

Life's whole arch, boring edifice;
kids at a loose end kick up stink
(want this want that, expecting it on a platter);
such kids do not know, perhaps,
that others died for them.
Fat, rich men do - they know it all,
and keep it under their hats.

Sacrifice

Past generations used to say,
it was done for them.

We say today
it was done for us.

Future generations will say,
it is done for them;

whereas the truth of it is,
that it just goes on being done.

D-Day
(A personal perspective)

The great machine took off
all vessels to the water
going one way across the Channel
forward - no turning back
engines droning relentlessly
sat there in your tunic
inside your operations unit - waiting
as time devours distance
in slow motion until - suddenly - bang!
your number's up
(E-boat, torpedo or something)
watery inferno
the world upside-down
confusion makes a mockery
of military calculation
nothing quite prepares you for this -
into the sea's cold blackness
no going back - this is what war is all about.

The telegram

Right through the war
we came to dread the telegram,
telegrams bore terrible news
sons and husbands killed
in action others lost -
gone forever without trace.

On the day in question,
our particular telegram,
missing on D-Day:
"I have to inform you with regret."

Life and love and war,
how you come through it all -
a sort of Russian roulette.

Portrait of victory
(Remembering: Jeannie Christina Lebby 1939-1945)

Posing for the camera,
two children stand with Union Jacks,
the elder, perhaps four or five years old,
screws up her face in a sort of smile,
the other, much younger, her flag draped
over the ground, her hand outstretched in
supplication, the eyes dazed, bewildered,
an expression on her face
which defies meagre words:
it is the end of the war, children;
tomorrow will be your world,
the world we have bequeathed to you,
sadly with no promise it won't all happen again.

It's over

It's over.

The news came through,
the war - it's over - and now?

We were told: "it's over" - the war - it's official.

We went out into the street to share the news,
"Isn't it wonderful?" said Mrs Smith.

I can't recall anything else,
just hearing the news,
and going out onto the street -

that's all I can remember
from the *greatest* day in our lives.

[John Vetterlein, aged nine at the time]

Warring on...

A military exercise,
they say on the radio fifty years on;

you question what's going on?

It's going on, it never stopped in fact;
warring's in the system,
no matter how we try to stop it, it goes on;
that's the way with addiction.

Remembrance

Remember, remember...
that time of year, cold November
(as it was that time in the trenches);
remember, remember,
recall, if you prefer - but learn?

This peculiar brand of nostalgia:
feel free to join the fine suited,
uniformed and decorated
at the Cenotaph;
the Cenotaph - a memorial for what?

They died for freedom,
they gave their lives for their country,
fought for democracy,
died for king and empire,
lost their lives defending the faith.

So much for the rhetoric:
many a soldier went forth
believing right was on his side;
more, possibly, in their thousands
went simply to join the battle.

Those who were on the spot and survived
will not need to be told to remember.
They have every right to hold us to account:
"We killed and got killed,
and since then nothing has changed."

Remember, remember...

Black Hole

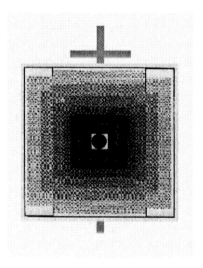

Why suffer'st thou thy sons, unburied yet
To hover on the dreadful shore of Styx?
Make way to lay them by their brethren.
There rest in silence as the dead are wont,
And sleep in peace, slain in your country's wars!
O sacred receptacle of my joys,
Sweet cell of virtue and nobility,
How many sons of mine hast thou in store,
That thou wilt never render to me more!

Titus Andronicus: William Shakespeare

Black Hole

The fist is mightier than the tongue, meaning
war will capsize us into oblivion - ultimately;
it is law, it would seem, binding us to aggressive conflict;

at pains to build, pain in destructive acts,
the edifice that is civilization has all the potential
for its own salvation, together with its downfall:
we take the latter course.

War feeds on the common ignorance,
our *missightedness* and vanities;
war is an outrage against the spirit,
war is the black hole of human endeavour.

***

The Cross

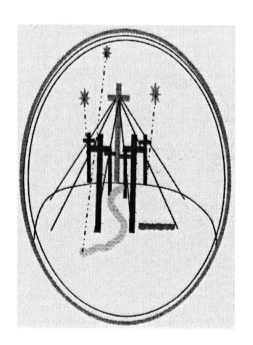

The Cross is a direct response to the most recent display of violence in the Balkans involving not only the quarrelling indigenous populations on the ground, but also the intervention by outside forces of distant nations using the most sophisticated apparatus of modern aerial warfare, ostensibly to bring some kind of stability to the region.

Quite how it is we think we can celebrate the Millennium at the close of a century which has been the most violent perpetrated by mankind defies understanding: two thousand years of mostly snubbing Christ.

John Vetterlein
1999 April 30

To the memory of Pierre Ceresole - true man of peace.

The Cross

The killing will only stop when we desist,
no instrument of war can achieve it,
the will has to come from within ourselves,
fighting evil with evil only fans the flames,
begets a greater evil; smashing tyrants in the face
bloods only bigger tyrants, for
the end and the means are one and the same;
Christ carried his cross, he did not throw it from him,
neither did he strike his executioners with it...

Christ, in death, offered the cross to us.

Pierre Ceresole

Pierre Ceresole was born at Lausanne, Switzerland, in 1879, the second youngest of a family of ten children. Here, at the time, the language was French, the chief religion, Protestant. At the age of seventeen, on one of his solitary walks in the Bois de Gantenaz, he experienced what he described as a "vision of Truth" which was to have a profound influence on the course he took in life.

Ceresole's father was a colonel in the Swiss Army and held other high ranking official posts. After a good standard education, Pierre Ceresole went on to study mechanical engineering, taking his doctorate from Zurich. Next he went to Göttingen to study physics and mathematics. By the time he returned to his native Switzerland, Ceresole was well qualified to take up a "safe" academic career. Instead, after a short term teaching mathematics, he went on to work his passage across the United States.

Ceresole's travels took him on to Hawaii, Japan, India and elsewhere. But he was no ordinary traveller, preferring to make his way in whatever employment he could get ranging from manual work to teaching.

Throughout his life Ceresole kept notebooks by him for his jottings of observation and reflection. Many of these notes, together with his letters, were published in French. A very useful and interesting publication in English appeared in 1954 under the title "For Peace and Truth", translated and edited by John W Harvey and Christina Yates.

Ceresole took a practical view of peace, aiming to live his *truth* at all costs, much of the cost to his own physical well-being (he was imprisoned many times for violating border restrictions, for example). Having lived through two world wars - he died on the 23rd October, 1945 - he was instrumental in setting up *Service Civil International*, a voluntary organization designed to foster peaceful, constructive projects across international boundaries.

J V

Reading about the perpetual quarrels, the savage hatreds in the Balkans, suddenly gripped by a picture of the extreme difficulty, in history, of being pacific, of the "scandal of pacifism", as you might say.

What! in a world like that, where man is so naturally given over to his profound, ferocious, murderous egoism, to his passions, - is that the world in which you can claim all of a sudden to lay down your arms, to renounce all your safeguards and the group guarantees which it has taken thousands of years to develop?

I see this, it comes home to me with sudden force. And the answer is Yes! It's like suddenly passing from the morbid passionate mentality of the lunatic living in a world of lunatics to the detached, absolutely different (totaliter aliter) attitude of the doctor who moves among such people and treats them.

The horrible, permanently poisoned atmosphere of the vendetta: I will injure you if you have injured me even if, in injuring you I injure myself still more; and to bring about a future that gets worse and worse: - this is the lunacy, the disease from which only Christian effort can save us. It is imperative at almost any price that someone should give in and not return blow for blow: and then equilibrium and peace can be re-established. It must be done with the greatest courage, the greatest calm.

Pierre Ceresole (1940)

***

DRESDEN PRE-ECHO

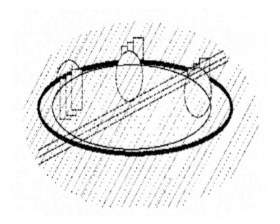

For God will Judah's cities build,
and he will Sion save,
That they may dwell therein, and it
in sure possession have.

Psalm LXIX (35)

Dresden pre-echo

Rachmaninoff in Dresden, 1926,
confronts the shambles of our musical thought
with his *Fourth Concerto*,
brings before us the grotesque destruction
perpetrated in the air raids of World War Two;
in the sudden crescendo of the second movement
I hear the razing to the ground of cities,
in the subsequent heaving, dragging tread through the orchestra
something of our attempt to right ourselves from the ashes;

but the music gives us no more release
than we give ourselves, violence
is too deeply woven into our psyche;

war is the only course we appear to understand;
a blighted intelligence outlived its purpose,
unless that purpose is to wipe out all civilization,
all art, all life from this wretched planet.

Rachmaninoff: *Piano Concerto in G minor, No. 4*

Rachmaninoff had not yet left Russia in April 1914 when he was reported to be working on a fourth concerto for piano. The war, which had just commenced, was said to have seriously affected his concentration to the extent that he temporarily abandoned the project.

In 1917 the unrest in Russia forced Rachmaninoff to leave his homeland. He went first to Scandinavia as a performing artist, eventually reaching the U.S.A. in November, 1918. From here he built his frenzied career as a pianoforte soloist of the highest rank - a treadmill life that he found best served his needs as an exile, a husband and father but, and this must never be overlooked, a composer of great integrity.

Rachmaninoff took up the composition of the *Fourth Concerto* in real earnest in 1926. This he did, initially, from his New York apartment. But the distractions there - this time more social and professional than political - were too great, and so he made his way to Europe where his family were again united. They rented a villa in a district of Dresden and it was from here that the concerto was finally completed. He wrote to Medtner (the concerto's dedicatee): "Just before leaving Dresden I received the copied piano score of my completed concerto. I glanced at its size - 110 pages - and was terrified."

The work was not well received from the start (indeed, some of the criticism was vitriolic) and once more, as had happened with the *First Symphony*, Rachmaninoff was despondent and put the concerto away. Some fourteen years later, and with yet another war in progress, Rachmaninoff returned to the concerto subjecting it to radical revision. This 1941 version is the one most frequently performed today. Both versions retain the essential mood, the perennial "Russian gloom" characteristic of much of the composer's output.

The *Fourth Concerto* is still generally regarded as the least successful, and by some (who should know better) the least workmanlike. For all the vicissitudes the concerto has been through it holds for the present writer a similar place to the *Third Symphony* - that is to say, it is to be rated as amongst Rachmaninoff's finest music.

White City

For me this poem, *White City**, represents a sort of culmination in my writing; it expresses as closely as anything I have done something of what I feel to be the bizarre whiff of human existence.

John Vetterlein, August 1998

Dedication: Mrs Elsie Smith**

White City

Rachmaninoff saw in Böcklin's *Isle of the Dead*
something so powerful, so arcane,
it brought out of him a masterpiece -
The Isle of the Dead.

Shortly after the Second World War ended,
when we were letting our hair down,
our next-door neighbours - one day -
took themselves off to White City
(for an event held there); in my child head
the name suggested a picture
as arcane in its way as Böcklin's painting,
a picture from memory of immediate
pre-war housing, concrete balconies,
wine, women and song, all hidden
beneath the glare of the searchlight,
deafened-out by the anti-aircraft gun.

*For those who are unfamiliar with London, White City is a district encompassing within a few hundred yards of one another: White City Stadium, West London Stadium, Hammersmith Hospital, Old Oak Common, Wormwood Scrubs, H.M.Prison (Wormwood Scrubs), and at the time of writing, The British Broadcasting Cooperation's Radio and Television Centres and a network of railways and roads including (now) Westway A40 (Motorway), and a great deal more.

**Mrs Elsie Smith, her husband and daughter Brenda (of about my age) were our neighbours at Redbridge throughout the period of the Second World War. Without a transfusion of this lady's blood serum, sought urgently in the small hours, it is unlikely my mother would have survived the birth of my brother Robert on 7 J

Postscript to the collection

When I embarked upon this project about eighteen months ago I have to admit to feeling pretty depressed about things in general and about the state of the world and its current wars in particular. I'm afraid nothing eases my sense of pessimism. Militarism is so much an inoperable ingrown toenail condition with us that I see no bright future for the inhabitants of this planet.

One of my first loves in music was Franz Schubert. A good deal of present-day research into the composer's life seems to want to paint him as a manic depressive. His life was tragically short-lived: he died in his thirty-first year. As a child during the Second World War when listening to the music of Schubert I identified in it a gloom of cosmic proportions.

I can end this collection of poems no more fittingly than by quoting from the notes (Walter Dürr 1982) accompanying a recording of Schubert's final *Mass in E flat* and written within weeks of his death. "Schubert could not believe in peace - even though by 1828, the year of the E flat Mass, Austria had enjoyed thirteen years of peace. But Metternich's peace was not Schubert's. The Mass stands as a document to the wretchedness of this world."

July 18 2006

Printed in the United Kingdom
by Lightning Source UK Ltd.
119319UK00002B/64-69